NUMBER KIT 1

What's that number?

Reading, writing and ordering numbers

All rights reserved. This book is sold subject to the condition that it shall not, by way of trade or otherwise, be lent, hired out or otherwise circulated without the publisher's prior consent in any form of binding or cover other than that in which it is published and without a similar condition, including this condition, being imposed upon the subsequent purchaser.

No part of this publication may be reproduced, stored in a retrieval system, or transmitted, in any form or by any means, electronic, mechanical, photocopying, recording or otherwise, without the prior permission of the publisher. This book remains copyright, although permission is granted to copy those pages labelled PHOTOCOPIABLE for classroom distribution and use only in the school which has purchased the book, or by the teacher who has purchased this book, and in accordance with the CLA licensing agreement. Photocopying permission is given for purchasers only and not for borrowers of books from any lending service.

British Library Cataloguing-in-Publication Data
A catalogue record for this book is available from the British Library.

ISBN 0-590-53581-1

Published by Scholastic Ltd
Villiers House
Clarendon Avenue
Leamington Spa
Warwickshire CV32 5PR

© 1996 Scholastic Ltd
123456789   6789012345

AUTHOR
Kim Connor

SERIES CONSULTANT
Sheila Ebbutt
Director of BEAM (Be A Mathematician) which is supported by Islington Council

CURRICULUM LINKS
Ian Gardner, Maths Curriculum Adviser, (England and Wales), Julie Parkin, with Edinburgh Centre for Mathematics Education (Scotland) and Michael Wallace (Northern Ireland)

The publishers wish to thank the following individuals and organisations for their invaluable help in developing the *Maths Focus* concept: Jayne de Courcy, Courcy Consultants; Dr Daphne Kerslake; West Sussex Maths Centre, West Sussex Institute; Oxfordshire Maths Centre; Edinburgh Centre for Mathematics Education; David Bell, Assistant Director for Education, Newcastle-upon-Tyne; Professor Geoffrey and Dr Julia Matthews

EDITORIAL TEAM
Angela Dewsbury and Jo Saxelby-Jennings

SERIES DESIGNER
Joy White

DESIGNERS
Blade Communications

COVER PHOTOGRAPH
© Scholastic Inc.

ILLUSTRATORS
Val Biro, Roma Bishop (John Martin & Artists), Sonia Canals, Debbie Clark (Simon Girling Assoc.), Trevor Dunton, Emma Holt (Sylvie Poggio), Claire James (Graham-Cameron), Lorna Kent, Derek Matthews, Chris Russell, Peter Read, Mick Reid (Peters, Fraser and Dunlop) and The Drawing Room.

POSTERMAT
Peter Read

Designed using Aldus Pagemaker
Processed by PAGES Bureau, Leamington Spa
Printed in Great Britain by Ebenezer Baylis & Son, Worcester and George Over, Rugby

© Material from the National Curriculum, Scottish 5–14 Guidelines and the Northern Ireland Curriculum is Crown copyright and is reproduced by permission of the Controller of HMSO, 1995.

CONTENTS

4	*MATHS FOCUS* OFFERS...
6	HERE'S THE MATHS
8	CURRICULUM LINKS
9	USING AND APPLYING GRID

DIAGNOSTIC ASSESSMENT
10	FRUIT AND VEG

ASSESSMENT DOUBLE-CHECK
14	NUMBER HUNT

REINFORCEMENT ACTIVITIES
16	COLLECT A NUMBER
18	NUMBERS ALL AROUND US
20	FISH AROUND A NUMBER
22	DOTTY NUMBERS
24	NEXT NUMBER
26	1, 2, 3, 4, 5
28	BOAT RACE
30	MISSING NUMBERS

ENRICHMENT ACTIVITIES
32	WHAT A HANDFUL!
34	WATCH THE NUMBERS
36	NUMBER LINES
38	ROCKET GAME
40	COUNT FORWARDS, COUNT BACK
42	DON'T MISS THE TRAIN!

RESOURCES
44	FISH AROUND A NUMBER
45	DOTTY NUMBERS CARDS
46	ROCKET GAME
47	DON'T MISS THE TRAIN
48	PHOTOCOPIABLE OF POSTERMAT

MATHS FOCUS

Maths Focus can be used to:

- ▶ assess children's knowledge and skills;
- ▶ offer reinforcement activities to develop understanding;
- ▶ provide enrichment activities to consolidate and extend the learning;
- ▶ develop skills and ability in using and applying mathematics.

DIFFERENTIATION

1 *Maths Focus* offers structured progression of content and skills through the Kits 1–5* and provides links with all UK national curricula. With a particular class or year group, you may use activities from more than one kit to cater for all ability levels. Each book focuses on a specific mathematical concept, with activities set in a range of contexts – including games, stories, problems, everyday situations and puzzles – so that children learn to use their mathematics flexibly and appropriately.

2 Assessment activities allow you to evaluate the children's ability to use and apply the mathematics they have learned.

3 Understanding is developed through two types of activity:
▶ **Reinforcement activities** – which increase children's confidence by concentrating on specific concept or skill and presenting the maths in a variety of contexts;
▶ **Enrichment activities** – which consolidate and extend children's learning in more open-ended contexts.

4 Extension ideas at the end of each activity offer ways for more able children to go further in their exploration of a concept.

*See inside back cover for overview of kits and curriculum coverage.

offers...

FLEXIBLE RESOURCE

Maths Focus can be used in a variety of ways to support your teaching of mathematics and your style of teaching, allowing you to use the activities with individuals, groups or the whole class.

Use **Maths Focus** activities alongside a published scheme to:
- develop children's understanding of specific concepts in a greater range of contexts;
- assess children's understanding of a concept, and then to support or extend it with differentiated activities;
- focus on the using and applying aspect of the mathematics curriculum.

If you don't use a published scheme use **Maths Focus**:
- as a core resource when planning your own scheme of work;
- to teach and assess specific concepts.

USING & APPLYING

Aspects of **Using and Applying** covered by each activity are given in the teacher's notes. To help with your planning, the grid on page 9 and the teachers' notes highlight how problem solving, communication and logical reasoning are built into each activity.

USING TALK

All teachers' notes pages offer questions you can ask children to encourage them to talk about what they are doing. Use the questions while they are working to focus their mathematical thinking or at the end of the activity to assess their level of understanding. Most pages also offer:
- **Here's the maths** – explanations of the maths included in the activity;
- **What to look for** – diagnostic pointers to help you to assess whether the child has achieved the mathematical aim of the activity;
- **More help needed** – ways to help children are who struggling with the activity.

ASSESSMENT

Maths Focus offers two types of assessment to be used when you feel appropriate to plan the best way forward for each child.

- You may want to use the **Diagnostic assessment** activity at the start of teaching a concept to establish the existing level of understanding. Alternatively, use it after some initial teaching, to provide a check on progress.

- The **Assessment double-check** allows you to assess the child's understanding of the concept as a whole, to see how their learning has progressed.

RANGE OF RESOURCES

Maths Focus kits come with a full-colour laminated postermat for each book. This flexible wipe-clean resource can be used with a number of the activities in its book and also as a general mathematics resource. Each book has a black and white photocopiable version of its postermat, to use with the activities and for permanent recording of the children's work. Extra postermats are available separately (see inside back cover).

The activities in each book are planned to use a range of mathematical resources, including counting apparatus, number lines and grids and calculators. Mental maths is emphasised throughout.

Numbers are all around us. Build on children's familiarity to give them a firm foundation in reading, writing and ordering numbers so that they can then later explore the number system with confidence.

Here's the maths…

Reading, writing and ordering numbers

What's involved

▶ From an early age children meet numbers in a variety of contexts. They see them on clock-faces, birthday cards, telephones, buses… . They hear them in songs, rhymes, stories, counting games… . As they begin to realise the significance of number in the world around them they start to use numbers as part of their spoken vocabulary. We need to make the most of these experiences, to start from what they already know.

▶ Children's early awareness of the numbers around them provides a strong basis for learning to read, write and order numbers. However, for this learning to be effective it needs to be nurtured in practical and meaningful activities so that the child develops full understanding and confident use of the numbers encountered.

▶ Children will be required to use number in many different contexts, applying their knowledge to various practical situations which involve objects. Eventually they will need to be able to deal with number as an abstract idea, not attached to any objects at all. This involves:
- knowing how to compare numerical sizes by pairing (one-to-one matching);
- knowing that the numerical size is not changed by moving the objects around (conservation of number);
- being able to use numerical size to put several sets into order;
- being able to measure the numerical size of a set by counting.

NUMBER NAMES UP TO 10 AND BEYOND

▶ Children need a range of activities which will allow them to acquire a confident knowledge of number names so that they can then use numbers effectively. They will be required to use this knowledge of number names and their symbols up to 10 and beyond in all areas of the curriculum. This could be through planned activities as well as spontaneous opportunities which arise in everyday situations, such as lining up at the door or a PE game.

▶ The maths activities which the children are involved with should also give them practice in forming numbers, for example, in the context of recording their work.

READING AND WRITING NUMBERS

▶ While children are learning to count and say the numbers, they also need experience of: watching you write the number; matching that number with the correct number card/tablet; reading the number.

▶ To develop their ability to write the numbers accurately give them opportunities to: write them in the air, in sand, with paint, with chalk; model them from Plasticine; trace over them from a number card and complete partially formed numbers.

CONSERVATION OF NUMBER

▸ Children need an awareness of the conservation of number if they are to realise that the position of objects in a set doesn't alter the number there are of them. So, for example, if one pencil is moved from a set of five pencils on a table to a different position on the table, the total number of pencils is still 5.

▸ It is important to use the correct vocabulary when talking to the children about this idea. Clearly, five pencils are not the *same* as five oranges, it is the 'fiveness' of the oranges which is the same as the 'fiveness' of the set of pencils. Also, make sure you use sets of different yet related objects, such as five different pieces of fruit, so that children realise that it is not the fact that the objects are identical which counts.

▸ Before children can confidently use the numbers in our number system they need considerable experience of sorting, matching, 1:1 correspondence, comparison and ordering of sets. Through this experience they should also develop confidence with the number names up to 10 and beyond.

▸ When children learn to count they learn a sequence of number words just as they might learn a nursery rhyme. While it is important that they learn this sequence - without it they won't be able to count - being able to recite numbers in order doesn't prove that they can actually count. They may be able to recite the sequence from 1 to 10 perfectly, but be unable to use this sequence to count a set of objects.

▸ Young children will often miss out objects when they count, count the same objects twice, or say the number names in a different rhythm to their pointing, so at the end of the count they will be uncertain as to exactly how many objects there are. Provide a range of varied practical activities to help the children to get to grips with these ideas. This practice will also help them to gain an understanding of conservation of number.

▸ As children's experience develops they will need to build up their confidence in reading and writing numbers. They will also need to be able to order numbers, since this skill provides the key to exploring and learning about our number system.

ORDERING NUMBERS

▸ When children learn the number names, they learn them in order, so they may know that 3 comes before 6, for example, just as C comes before F in the alphabet. However, there is an important distinction between the order of letters in our alphabet and the order of our numbers: the ordering of the letters is arbitrary, but a set of three objects has fewer members than a set of six objects, so 3 comes before 6 in the order of the numbers.

▸ Children need lots of experience in ordering sets of objects – from the one with fewest members to the one with the most – rather than just ordering numerals, so that they understand this distinction. Comparison involves two sets of objects. Ordering involves three or more sets.

KEY FACTS

The activities in this books cover four main learning strands of number:
▸ counting;
▸ number names up to 10 and beyond;
▸ recognising symbols from 0 to 9 and beyond;
▸ ordering numbers.

KEY WORDS

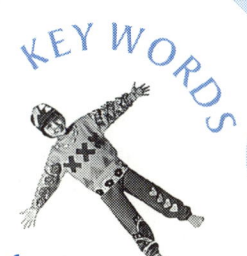

fewer
more
less
same as
next
before
after
1st, 2nd, 3rd, 4th, 5th
last
a guess
a count

WHAT'S THAT NUMBER
MATHS FOCUS – NUMBER KIT 1

Curriculum links

This chart outlines the particular strands and statements from each of the UK curriculum documents for maths that apply to the content of this book.

The processes outlined opposite show how this maths is applied to a range of contexts and how outcomes are reported.

MATHEMATICS IN THE NATIONAL CURRICULUM (ENGLAND AND WALES)

This book covers the following statements from the Key Stage 1 Programme of Study for Number:
▶ Pupils should be given opportunities to:
• develop flexible methods of working with number, orally and mentally;
• encounter numbers greater than 1000 (discussion);
• use a variety of practical resources and contexts;
• use calculators as a means to explore number;
• record in a variety of ways, including ways that relate to their mental work. (1a, b, c, d [part] and e)

Pupils should be taught to:
▶ Developing an understanding of place value
• count orally up to 10 and beyond, knowing the number names; count collections of objects, checking the total; count in steps of different sizes...; recognise sequences, including odd and even numbers;
• read, write and order numbers, initially to 10, progressing up to 1000, developing an understanding that the position of a digit signifies its value; begin to approximate larger numbers to the nearest 10 or 100. (2a and b)
▶ Solving numerical problems
• begin to check answers in different ways..., and gain a feel for the appropriate size of an answer. (4d)

MATHEMATICS 5–14 (SCOTTISH GUIDELINES)

This book covers the following strands of the Attainment Outcome Number, Money and Measurement:
▶ Range and type of numbers:
• **Work with:** whole numbers 0 to 20 (count, order, read/write statements, display on calculator) (Level A).

NORTHERN IRELAND CURRICULUM FOR MATHEMATICS

This book covers the following strand of Number from the Programme of Study for Mathematics at Key Stage 1:
▶ Understanding number and number notation
Pupils should have opportunities to:
(b) read, write and order whole numbers, initially to 10.

WHAT'S THAT NUMBER?
MATHS FOCUS – NUMBER KIT 1

Using and applying

All of the activities in **Maths Focus** involve applying mathematics. This chart will help you to identify which strands of Using and Applying Mathematics are part of each activity. Problem-solving and Enquiry (Scottish 5–14 Guidelines) and Processes (NI Curriculum) are also addressed through these statements.

Activities	Problem Solving	Communication	Logical Reasoning
DIAGNOSTIC ASSESSMENT			
Fruit and veg	Work independently. Work systematically. Check the answers.	Talk about this work. Record clearly.	Able to use the information given on the activity sheets to carry out the task.
ASSESSMENT DOUBLE-CHECK			
Number hunt	Know how to tackle the problem. Work systematically. Complete the task.	Record clearly. Explain his or her methods	Know what information is needed to solve the problem. Able to collect and use this information effectively.
REINFORCEMENT ACTIVITIES			
Collect a number	Work independently and with accuracy.	Record appropriately. Talk about the work.	Understand that the 'fiveness' of the oranges is the same as the 'fiveness' of the pencils.
Numbers all around us	Show an interest in the numbers. Select and use the objects required.	Talk about observations. Express ideas clearly.	Make a connection between a number and its meaning or use in everyday contexts.
Fish around a number	Recognise when a numeral is 'the wrong way round'. Self-correct work.	Talk about the way in which a number is formed.	Find and use each time the starting point for each numeral.
Dotty numbers	Check recording and ensure there is no number repetition. Complete the task independently.	Talk about work Explain the rule. Write the numerals clearly.	Count the dots accurately. Give the correct number name to each set of dots.
Next number	Think about the number sequences involved. Create other ways of playing.	Say the names of the numbers in sequence. Use vocabulary such as next, after. Talk about what is happening to the numbers.	Guess what the next number (or numbers) will be. Describe the number patterns found.
1, 2, 3, 4, 5	Work systematically. Check results.	Use mathematical language such as first, next, last and so on. Explain what she or he is doing.	Predict 'the next number'. Know how to put numbers in the correct order.
Boat race	Organise the work independently.	Use the words 1st, 2nd, 3rd and so on with understanding.	Locate a boat using position.
Missing numbers	Use the first caterpillar to check answers. Work systematically.	Explain how to play the game to someone else. Talk about the position of the numbers.	Anticipate the next number.
ENRICHMENT ACTIVITIES			
What a handful!	Think about 'why' they are getting particular results.	Explain the difference between a guess and a count.	Make reasonable guesses.
Watch the numbers	Understand the idea of the game in order to make a different version.	Talk about the numerals.	Identify and talk about which are the larger/smaller numbers.
Number lines	Complete the task. Devise a different number line.	Discuss the numerals.	Discuss number patterns.
Rocket game	Play the game correctly.	Talk about the numbers and direction of the move.	Be aware of the connection between moving forwards and '+' and moving backwards and '–'.
Count forwards, count back	Apply own ideas to the task. Extend work.	Talk about the work and explain ideas clearly.	Choose equipment to make their own game and use it appropriately
Don't miss the train!	Draw the correct number of compartments. Record clearly and discuss recording used.	Discuss the work.	

WHAT'S THAT NUMBER?
MATHS FOCUS – NUMBER KIT 1

TALK ABOUT

◗ 'How many apples are you putting on the market stall?'

◗ 'How do you know that you have drawn the right number of oranges?'

◗ 'Which bag has the most items in it?'

◗ 'Which bag has the fewest items in it?'

DIAGNOSTIC ASSESSMENT

Fruit and veg

Key aims

◗ To discover how confident a child is about:
- recognising and reading numerals;
- recording pictorially and in writing;
- counting.

What you need

◗ 1 activity sheet 'Fruit and veg 1' per child
◗ 1 activity sheet 'Fruit and veg 2' per child
◗ pencils and coloured crayons
◗ scissors

Organisation

◗ Before giving out the activity sheets, write the numbers from 0 to 10 on the bags of fruit and veg in a different arrangement on each sheet so each child can't copy from the person next to him.

◗ If possible, enlarge the 'Fruit and veg 1' sheets to A3 to increase the children's drawing space.

The activity

◗ Give out the activity sheets and explain that their empty market stall needs to be filled with fruit and veg ready for customers to come and buy. Tell the children to read the number in each of their bags and draw that number of fruit or veg on their market stall. You may want to demonstrate using an extra sheet.

◗ When you are sure the children know what to do leave them to work on their own.

◗ If a child completes this activity sheet easily, give and explain individually the activity sheet 'Fruit and veg 2'. Explain that the bags show the number of each fruit or veg bought by one of the customers (a different item in each bag).

◗ Explain that they must count how many are in each bag and write the number in the box – show them where. They can then cut out the bags and put them in order.

Where next?

◗ If the children are lacking in confidence, you may want to give them some small cubes or counters to see if they can carry out the activities with the help of apparatus.

◗ If the child completes both activity sheets easily, you will need to try an assessment at a higher level.

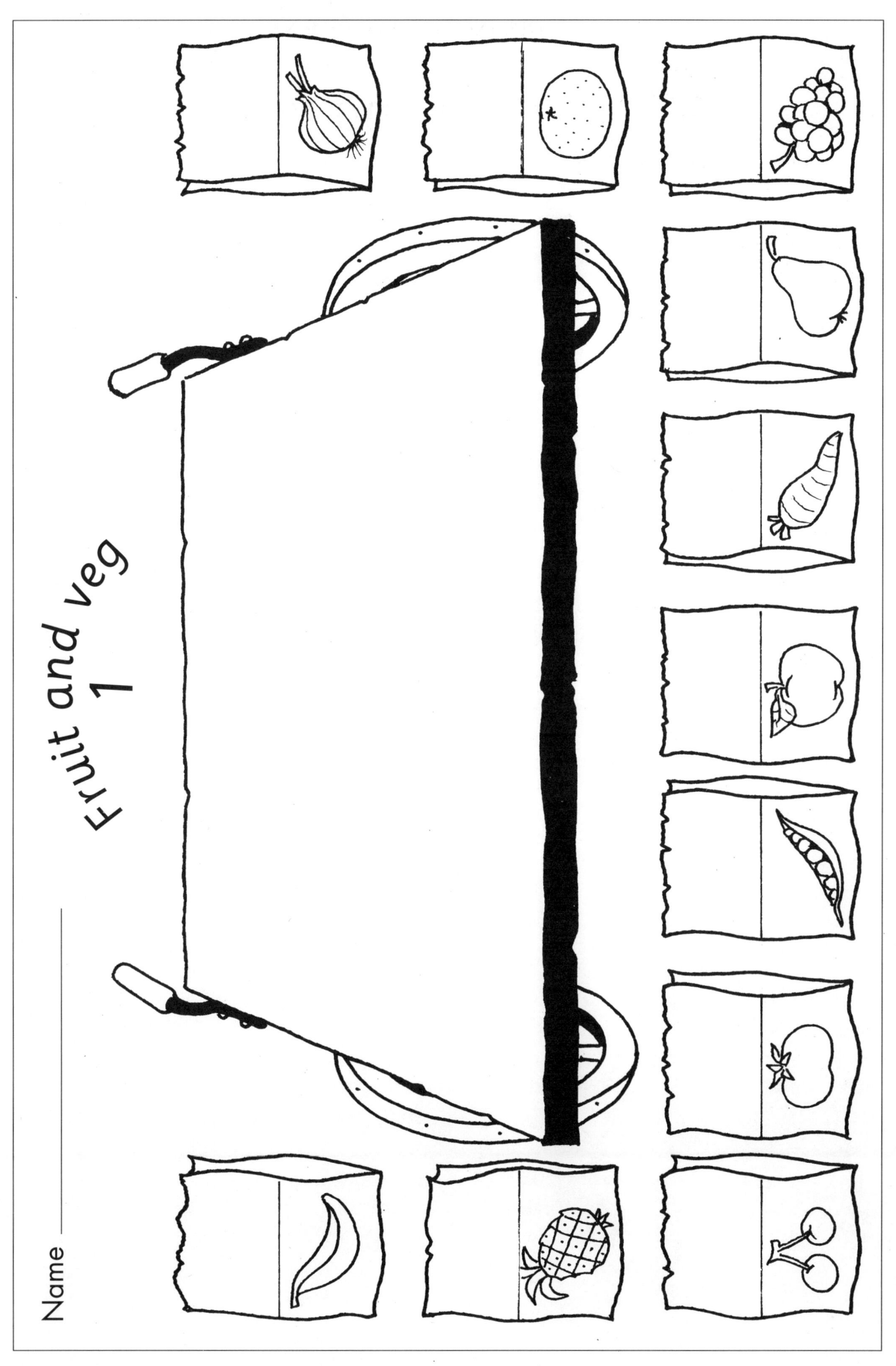

Fruit and veg 1

Name _____

PHOTOCOPIABLE

WHAT'S THAT NUMBER?
MATHS FOCUS – NUMBER KIT 1

11

ASSESSING, USING & APPLYING

PROBLEM SOLVING
◗ Can the child:
• work independently?
• work systematically?
• check the answers?
COMMUNICATION
◗ Can the child:
• talk about this work?
• record clearly?
LOGICAL REASONING
◗ Is the child able to use the information given on the sheets to carry out the task?

DIAGNOSTIC ASSESSMENT

Assessing understanding

◗ Look for the following to indicate that the children are ready for **Enrichment Activities**. They may:
• read the numerals with confidence and tell you confidently how many of each fruit and veg are to be put on the stall or are in the bags;
• carry out the task independently;
• record clearly and accurately using drawing and writing;
• show that they know how to check and correct their work;
• discuss which fruit or veg there is most or least of on both activity sheets.

◗ Look for the following to indicate that the children are in need of further work on reading, writing and ordering numbers. They may:
• lack confidence in carrying out the task, repeatedly ask questions or for reassurance;
• be unable to interpret the pictorial information given to them on the activity sheets;
• have difficulty counting;
• be unable to record accurately or consistently;
• be unable to put the numbers in order;
• be unable to tell you which fruit and veg there is most or least of;
• have difficulty explaining their work.

Children who need more help

◗ Children who do not understand the activity need to return to practical work using objects, such as the **Reinforcement activity** 'Collect a number'.

◗ Children who cannot read the numerals accurately and consistently could go on to the **Reinforcement activity** 'Numbers all around us'.

◗ Children who cannot write numerals accurately and consistently could go on to the **Reinforcement activities** 'Fish around a number' and 'Dotty numbers'.

◗ Children who cannot put the numbers in order could go on to the **Reinforcement activities** 'Next number', '1, 2, 3, 4, 5', 'Boat race' or 'Missing numbers'.

WHAT'S THAT NUMBER?
MATHS FOCUS – NUMBER KIT 1

Name _____

Fruit and veg 2

PHOTOCOPIABLE

WHAT'S THAT NUMBER?
MATHS FOCUS – NUMBER KIT 1

13

ASSESSING, USING & APPLYING

PROBLEM SOLVING
◗ Does the child:
• know how to tackle the problem?
• work systematically?
• complete the task?

COMMUNICATION
◗ Does the child:
• record clearly?
• explain his or her methods?

LOGICAL REASONING
◗ Does the child know what information is needed to solve the problem?
◗ Can the child collect and use this information effectively?

ASSESSMENT DOUBLE-CHECK

Number hunt

Key aims
◗ To assess if the child can:
• carry out the task independently;
• apply his or her knowledge to solve the problem;
• read, write and order numbers accurately.

What you need
◗ 1 activity sheet per child
◗ 1 set of cards per child (see 'Organisation')
◗ pens/pencils

Organisation
◗ Make a set of cards for each child displaying a mixture of numerals and dots for a number range, such as 0–10 or 0–20, according to the ability level of each child – start with the cards on page 45. Use a different colour for each set.

| 1 | 2 | ∴ | 4 | ∷ | 6 | 7 | ⁝⁝ |

◗ Remove between two and five cards from each set and hide the rest around the classroom.
◗ Use this assessment activity at any time with different numbers, to see how each child's understanding has progressed.

The activity
◗ Tell each child the colour of her set of cards, how many cards have been hidden and how many are missing.
◗ Ask them to find and record their hidden numbers from around the classroom and then discover which numbers are missing. Show them where to record this on their sheet.

Assessing understanding
◗ Look for an ability to:
• carry out the task independently;
• organise the work;
• use a method to solve the problem;
• write numerals accurately and clearly;
• order the numbers.

Children who need more help
◗ If the children do not show confidence at this stage, they will need further **Reinforcement activities** before they tackle problems set in less visual contexts or using larger numbers.

WHAT'S THAT NUMBER?
MATHS FOCUS – NUMBER KIT 1

Name _____

Number hunt

Numbers I've found...

Finding out which numbers are missing.

The missing numbers are:

REINFORCEMENT ACTIVITY

Collect a number

Key aims
- To practise counting objects.
- To develop recording skills.
- To develop understanding of the conservation of number.

What you need
- variety of everyday objects from around the classroom
- 1 activity sheet per child
- pencils and coloured crayons

Organisation
- This activity can be used with a whole class over a period of time or with individual children or groups to give extra practice. You may want to put the objects on a central resource table if you think having the children collect them will be too disruptive for the rest of the class.

The activity
- Write on each child's activity sheet a number from 1 to 5 that they need particular practice with, or from between 5 and 10 if they have done this activity before using numbers up to 5. Give out the sheets and ask the children to collect various objects of that many in number from around the room to bring back to their table to record by drawing and writing.

5 cubes 5 pencils 5 books

- Encourage the children to use their own ways of counting. Between them they may suggest: touching each object; pushing each object along; matching to four corks, for example; picking up and keeping in their hand; just by looking.

Extension ideas
- Think of different ways to record this activity, such as sticking down the objects on to card.
- Make individual books of their numbers or together make a big class book. The book should show different sets of that number of objects, for example, a picture of five apples.
- Have a practical classroom display of a particular number. The children then need to keep a check to ensure that there are, for example, four of each object still on the table.

USING & APPLYING

PROBLEM SOLVING
- Work independently and with accuracy.

COMMUNICATION
- Record appropriately.
- Talk about the work.

LOGICAL REASONING
- Realise that the 'fiveness' of the oranges is the same as the 'fiveness' of the pencils.

TALK ABOUT
- 'Which objects have you collected so far?'
- 'How many pencils have you got?'
- 'Which have you got most of, books or buttons?'
- 'Can you think of different ways to count the objects?'

HERE'S THE MATHS
- When you ask the children which object they have most of, some may still think that there are more books than buttons, for example, because they look bigger. They will need help seeing that there are the same number of objects in each set. They need to realise it is the 'fiveness' which makes the sets the same – if 5 is their number.

WHAT TO LOOK FOR
- Can the child organise her counting by moving the objects or pointing systematically?
- Can the child count consistently, not leaving any objects out?

MORE HELP NEEDED
- Children who are inconsistent with their counting need more experience counting things, in a real context. They may need help with organising the counting.

WHAT'S THAT NUMBER?
MATHS FOCUS – NUMBER KIT 1

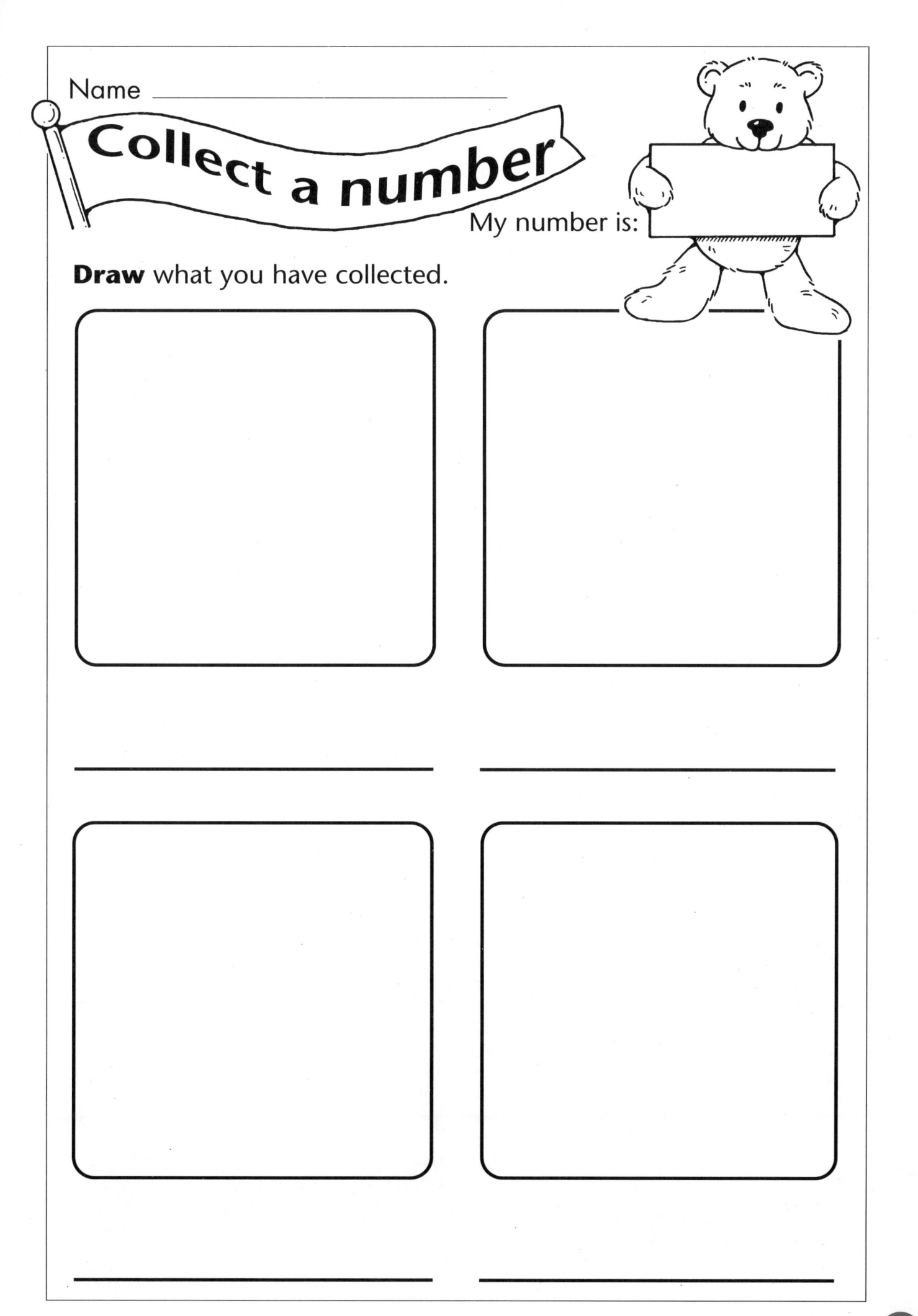

Name _____

Collect a number

My number is:

Draw what you have collected.

PHOTOCOPIABLE

WHAT'S THAT NUMBER?
MATHS FOCUS – NUMBER KIT 1

17

REINFORCEMENT ACTIVITY

Numbers all around us

Key aims
- To develop an awareness of numerals around us.
- To draw attention to the formation of numbers.

What you need
- variety of everyday objects showing numerals
- 1 activity sheet per child
- drawing and colouring pencils

Organisation
- Objects with numbers on in your classroom could include rulers, stop-watches, classroom clock, number lines, thermometers, measuring jugs, children's clothes, classroom door, pens and pencils, books with numbers in.
- Make sure you have examples of objects which show different ways of writing 4:

4   4   4   4

The activity
- Encourage the children to think about numbers in the classroom, at home or in the street, such as a street door, a telephone or a bus.
- Ask individuals to go around the classroom and bring back an object which shows a number or numbers. Continue this, collecting the objects on a table. You may want to introduce objects *you* have collected which have numbers on.
- Talk about the shape, size and colour of the numerals.
- Give out the activity sheets and talk about the two objects shown. Ask the children to fill in the numbers on each object on their sheet. Then let them choose some objects from the collection to look at carefully, draw and copy the numbers.
- Encourage them to continue on the back of their sheet.

Extension ideas
- Take the class for a walk around the block or along your local high street to look at and record the numbers they see around them. Then make a classroom display.
- Set up a role play area in your classroom which features many numbers, such as a shop, a post office or a travel agents.
- Look at numerals in other languages, for example, 6 in the Bengali system, how the Romans wrote 3 and so on.

USING & APPLYING

PROBLEM SOLVING
- Show an interest in the numbers.
- Select and use the objects required.

COMMUNICATION
- Talk about observations.
- Express ideas clearly.

LOGICAL REASONING
- Make a connection between a number and its meaning or use in everyday contexts.

TALK ABOUT
- 'Why do some things have numbers on?'
- 'Does the 5 on the shoe look the same as the 5 on the calculator?'
- 'Is there only one way to write the number 4?'
- 'Can you see an object which has just one number on its own? What about two numbers together? A lot of numbers?'

HERE'S THE MATHS
- When you ask the children to look for objects with two and more numbers together you will begin their awareness of 'digit' even though they are not talking directly about what a digit is, in the context of place value.
- It is important to relate children's experience of numbers to their lives. Children will meet large numbers, on buses, in shops and so on – make use of these experiences.

WHAT TO LOOK FOR
- Can the child say things about her numbers?
- Can the child read the numbers?

MORE HELP NEEDED
- Some children may need more work on simple numeral recognition.

WHAT'S THAT NUMBER?
MATHS FOCUS – NUMBER KIT 1

Name _____

Numbers all around us

Write the numbers on:

Draw some other things that have numbers.

PHOTOCOPIABLE

REINFORCEMENT ACTIVITY

Fish around a number

Key aim
◗ To practise forming numerals from 0 to 9.

What you need
◗ 1 activity sheet per child
◗ 1 'Fish around a number' resource sheet per child (see page 44)
◗ scissors
◗ card
◗ coloured pens

Introduction
◗ Use a writing board to model how to write each number while the children watch. As you form the number, talk about where to begin writing and which direction to follow. Encourage the children to write each number in the air as you model and discuss it.
◗ Ask individual children to come up and try to write the numbers, saying the starting point and direction.

The activity
◗ Give out the activity sheets and talk about the names of the numbers. Take each number in turn and ask the children to trace around it on their sheet using their index finger.
◗ Explain that they are going to cut out the little fish on the sheet and 'swim' it around each number. They may need help cutting the fish out accurately; it can then be backed on to card. Show them how to place and 'swim' their fish in the number by carefully pushing and guiding it round.
◗ After plenty of careful practice, they can draw in the route the fish takes. This can be done many times within the same number using different coloured pens.

Extension Ideas
◗ Explore writing numbers using a variety of mediums such as sand (wet and dry), Plasticine (using a tool), chalk, crayon or paint.
◗ Give the children cut-outs of numerals to cover with various materials such as cotton wool, small sticks, feathers and so on, to make feely numbers for a display.
◗ Place numbers cut out from card, in turn into a feely box. Each child feels the number in the box, describes its shape and guesses which number it is.

USING & APPLYING

PROBLEM SOLVING
◗ Recognise when a numeral is 'the wrong way round'.
◗ Self-correct work.
COMMUNICATION
◗ Talk about the way in which a number is formed.
LOGICAL REASONING
◗ Find and use each time the starting point for each numeral.

TALK ABOUT

◗ 'Where should the fish start with this number?'
◗ 'Which direction does the fish take for this number?'
◗ 'Which numbers have got straight lines?'
◗ 'Which numbers have got bends or curves?'
◗ 'Which numbers have got straight lines and curves?'
◗ 'Where should the fish start for the number 3? 7? 9?...'

HERE'S THE MATHS

◗ Physically tracing numerals with their fingers in this way helps children to connect with how they are written.

WHAT TO LOOK FOR

◗ Can the child form all the numerals in the correct way?

MORE HELP NEEDED

◗ Many children form their numerals in the reverse way that they should be written. They will need plenty of practical experience to reinforce the correct way of writing the numerals so that it begins to come naturally.

WHAT'S THAT NUMBER?
MATHS FOCUS – NUMBER KIT 1

Name _____

Fish around a number

PHOTOCOPIABLE

WHAT'S THAT NUMBER?
MATHS FOCUS – NUMBER KIT 1

21

USING & APPLYING

PROBLEM SOLVING
- Check recording and ensure there is no number repetition.
- Complete the task independently.

COMMUNICATION
- Talk about work.
- Explain the rule.
- Write the numerals clearly.

LOGICAL REASONING
- Count the dots accurately.
- Give the correct number name to each set of dots.

TALK ABOUT

- 'How can you check whether you have already had that number?'
- 'How do you know you have counted all the dots?'
- 'Have you written the numbers the right way round?'

HERE'S THE MATHS

- This activity gives practice in associating the numerals with the quantity. It also encourages children to build up a mental image of a number by looking at the pattern of dots on the dice.

WHAT TO LOOK FOR

- Can the child associate the right pattern of dots with the numeral?
- Does the child recognise if they have had that dot arrangement before?

MORE HELP NEEDED

- Give children who are finding the counting unmanageable a dice which has up to three dots only.
- Children who have difficulty counting the dots and cannot see the quantity by recognising the dot arrangement need more experience of counting sets of objects, matching one-to-one.

REINFORCEMENT ACTIVITY

Dotty numbers

Key aims
- To practise and develop counting skills.
- To begin to connect a set of dots to a numeral.
- To develop recording skills.

What you need
- 1–6 dice per child
- 1 activity sheet per child
- spare paper
- pens/pencils
- scissors

Introduction
- Look at a dice with the children and together count the number of dots on each side.

The activity
- Talk through the activity sheet. Using a spare sheet, have a go yourself to show them what you want them to do: throw the dice, draw the dots in the first box on the sheet and write the corresponding number beside it.
- Explain that the one rule is *that they must record a different number each time.* So if they throw a number they've already had they should ignore it and throw again.

Extension ideas
- The children could try to make their own 1–6 dice. Give them cards cut into squares, circles and triangles so that they have to choose what to use. Provide them with lots of examples of cubes for them to handle. Encourage them to draw on the dots before they stick the squares together with tape to make the cube for their dice.
- Repeat the activity using two dice and three dice, extending the number of dots they have to count and record.
- Look at the pattern of dots on a dice for the number 5. Do the same for other numbers.
- Use the 'Dotty numbers' cards on page 45 to make and play a Pelmanism (pairs) game to take home.

---

22 WHAT'S THAT NUMBER?
MATHS FOCUS – NUMBER KIT 1

Name _____

Dotty numbers

Throw your dice.

Draw the dots ...   then **write** the number.   **Draw** the dots ...   then **write** the number.

PHOTOCOPIABLE

WHAT'S THAT NUMBER?
MATHS FOCUS – NUMBER KIT 1

USING & APPLYING

PROBLEM SOLVING
- Think about the number sequences involved.
- Create other ways of playing.

COMMUNICATION
- Say the names of the numbers in the sequence.
- Use correct vocabulary such as *next, after*.
- Talk about what is happening to the numbers.

LOGICAL REASONING
- Guess what the next number (or numbers) will be.
- Describe the number patterns found.

TALK ABOUT

- 'What number comes after 3?'
- 'Here is 5... What comes next?'
- 'What is happening to the numbers?'
- 'Can you see a pattern?'
- 'What is 6 and 1 more?'

HERE'S THE MATHS

- Encourage the children to see the pattern to the sequence of '1 more'.

WHAT TO LOOK FOR

- Can the child follow the number sequence and know what comes next?
- Can the child see and talk about the pattern involved?

MORE HELP NEEDED

- Children who are having difficulty following the sequence of the numbers need simple counting activities, to become more familiar with what number comes next.

REINFORCEMENT ACTIVITY

Next number

Key aim
- To develop knowledge of and ability to think about the sequence of numbers.

What you need
- 1–10 number cards (see resource sheet on page 45)
- pens/pencils
- 1 activity sheet per child

Introduction
- Ask the children to form a circle with everyone kneeling down. Ask one child to stand up – count 1... then the next child – count 2... then the next child – count 3... and so on.
- With everyone standing, count around the circle, each child 'saying' the next number. Do this a few times.
- Ask every other child to kneel down, then count around the circle missing out the number of each child kneeling down. Encourage the children to count in their head; if they find this difficult they could mouth the number of the child kneeling.

The activity
- Spread out the number cards face up. Ask the children to name the numbers they can see.
- Explain that they are going to play a game which is like the circle game using cards. Shuffle the cards and deal them out.
- Players hold the cards in their hand so no one can see them.
- The player with number 1 takes the first turn by laying this card out on the table face up for everyone to see. The player on the left looks to see if she has 'the next number' and lays it on the table or misses a turn if she hasn't got it.
- Play continues until the number sequence is complete.
- When they have played a few times give out the activity sheets. Talk about how the children kneeling down are not showing their number. Let them fill in the missing numbers.

Extension ideas
- Extend the number cards to 20 or 30 and let the children play the game again.
- Play the game going backwards, with the highest card put down first.
- Play the game counting in 2s – the pattern will be odd numbers. Now try counting backwards in 2s (even numbers).
- Pair the children up to make a number line on the postermat (or page 48 for a permanent record). Starting with the number 1, the children take it in turns to write 'the next number' and keep going as far as they can.

---

24 WHAT'S THAT NUMBER?
MATHS FOCUS – NUMBER KIT 1

Name _____

Next number

Write in the numbers of the children kneeling down.

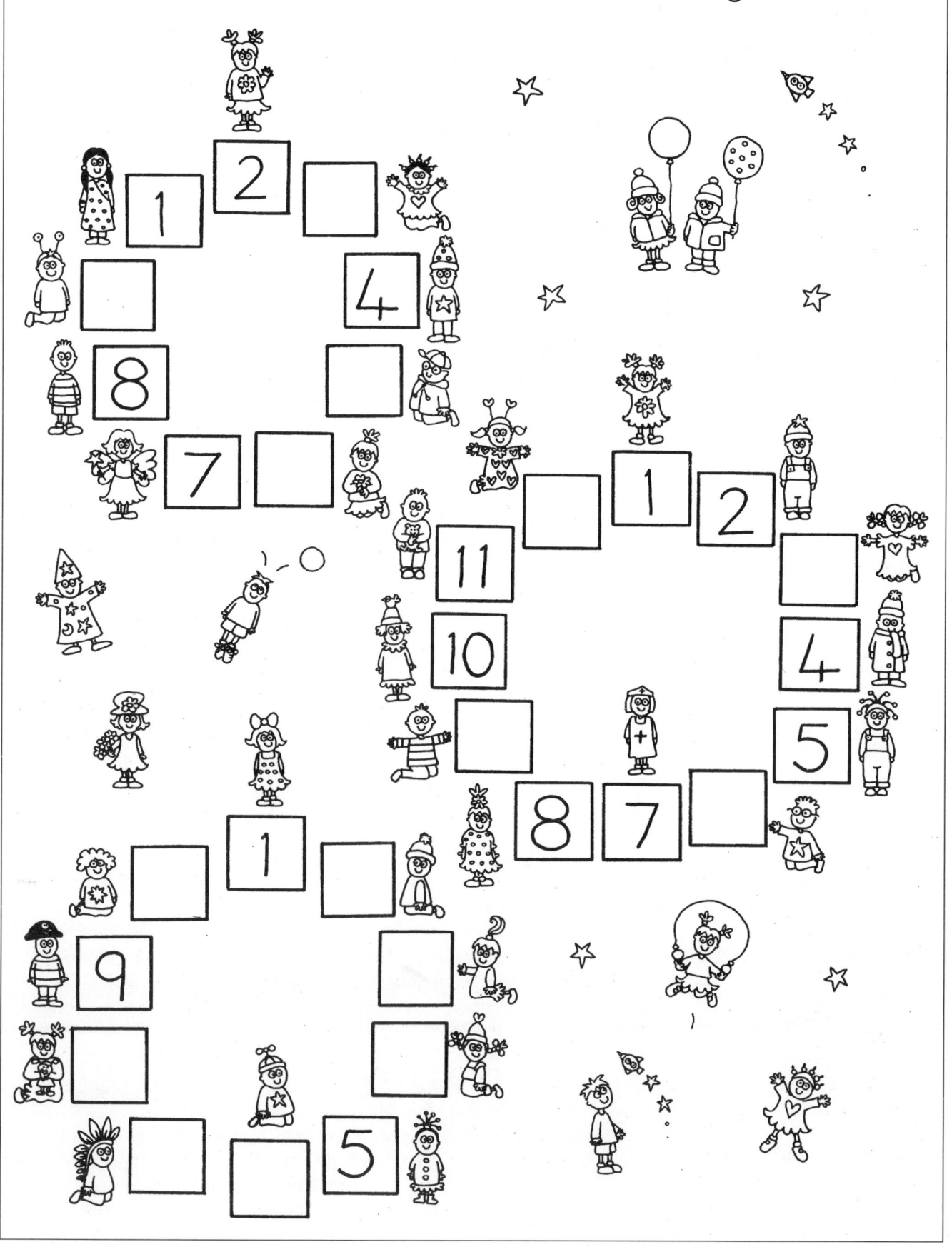

PHOTOCOPIABLE

WHAT'S THAT NUMBER?
MATHS FOCUS – NUMBER KIT 1

25

USING & APPLYING

PROBLEM SOLVING
◗ Work systematically.
◗ Check results.
COMMUNICATION
◗ Use mathematical language such as *first, next, last*.
◗ Explain what he or she is doing.
LOGICAL REASONING
◗ Predict 'the next number'.
◗ Know how to put numbers in the correct order.

TALK ABOUT

◗ 'How do you write 3? Which way does 5 go?'
◗ 'How can you check that you haven't written a number twice?'
◗ 'How do you know that none of the fish are missing?'
◗ 'Which number comes next?'
◗ 'When you put the fish in order, which side do you start from and why?'
◗ 'If I cover up one of your fish how can you find out which number it is?'

HERE'S THE MATHS

◗ Children need to use their existing knowledge of numbers to put the fish in the correct sequence.

WHAT TO LOOK FOR

◗ Can the child write the numbers to 10?
◗ Can the child put the numbers in order?

MORE HELP NEEDED

◗ Suggest to children who have difficulty counting their fish, that they put a counter on each fish as they count it.
◗ Children who have difficulty putting the fish in order, need more experience of saying numerals in order in class counting songs and rhymes.

REINFORCEMENT ACTIVITY

1, 2, 3, 4, 5

Key aims
◗ To reinforce the writing of numbers 1–10.
◗ To reinforce the ordering of numbers 1–10.

What you need
◗ 1 activity sheet per child
◗ colouring pencils or crayons
◗ scissors
◗ glue
◗ strips of blue paper – 1 per child

Introduction
◗ Sing the song '1, 2, 3, 4, 5, Once I caught a fish alive…' with the class, letting them use their fingers to show the numbers in the song. Alternatively, have children standing up – 1, then another 1 to make 2 and so on – to count the numbers as you sing.
◗ You may want to have the words written out on a big sheet of paper for the children to follow, depending on their ability.

The activity
◗ Give out the activity sheets and count the number of fish with them.
◗ Ask the children to write one number on each fish, from 1 to 10 in the circle on the fish.
◗ Check that they all write the numbers correctly and only one of each number.
◗ Now ask the children to colour in each fish, without colouring the number circle, and cut the fish cards out.
◗ When they have finished, return to the group and ask them to make sure they all have 10 fish and then to find fish number 1.
◗ Ask them to place this on their strip of blue paper and to then put the rest of the fish in number order.
◗ When they have all finished, get them to check each other's work – watch them while they do this. They can then glue down the fish to make a permanent record of the activity – a 1–10 number line.

Extension ideas
◗ Put the fish in order backwards.
◗ Extend their fish number line – some will want to start again from 1 to help them with the ordering, while others will be able to carry on from 10 on their existing number line.
◗ Make up their own song using their fish.

WHAT'S THAT NUMBER?
MATHS FOCUS – NUMBER KIT 1

Name _____

1, 2, 3, 4, 5

PHOTOCOPIABLE

WHAT'S THAT NUMBER?
MATHS FOCUS – NUMBER KIT 1

27

REINFORCEMENT ACTIVITY

Boat race

Key aims
◗ To focus on the order and position of numbers.
◗ To give experience of first, second, third, fourth, fifth.

What you need
◗ 1 activity sheet per child
◗ colouring pencils or crayons
◗ scissors
◗ 1 A3 piece of blue paper per child

Introduction
◗ Stories involving races would make a good background for this activity, such as Aesops tale of the hare and the tortoise. The naming of the years for the Chinese new year is another good one.

The activity
◗ Give out the activity sheets and ask the children to colour in each boat a different colour and cut them out.
◗ Give them a sheet of A3 paper each and tell them to stick down their boats as if they are in a race. You may want to talk about races with them first if you haven't used a 'race' story to introduce the activity.
◗ Next, they colour the rosette with 1st on in the colour of their winning boat and cut it out and stick it on the boat. Repeat this with all of the rosettes.

Extension ideas
◗ Use everyday classroom opportunities to talk about 1st, 2nd, 3rd and so on, such as lining up for playtime.
◗ Let each child paint a picture of a boat with their name on to make a classroom display of a boat race with large rosettes indicating the positions of the boats. If the boats are attached with drawing pins the winning order can be changed.

USING & APPLYING

PROBLEM SOLVING
◗ Organise the work independently.
COMMUNICATION
◗ Use the words 1st, 2nd, 3rd and so on with understanding.
LOGICAL REASONING
◗ Locate a boat using position.

TALK ABOUT
◗ 'What colour is your 1st boat? And your 3rd? Your 4th?'
◗ 'What number is your last boat?'
◗ 'Where did your green boat come in the race?'
◗ 'If I cover this blue boat with my hand can you tell me where it is in the race?'
◗ 'Can you tell me the winning order of your boat race?'
◗ 'Who was 1st, 2nd, 3rd coming into the class today? How can we record this?'

HERE'S THE MATHS
◗ Some children may be unfamiliar with the language of ordinal number involved in this activity, especially beyond first and second. If this activity is the first time they have come across this, then you need to follow it up with lots of practical day-to-day classroom activities reinforcing the concept.

WHAT TO LOOK FOR
◗ Can the child describe the order of the boats using ordinal number languag such as *first*, *second* and so on?

WHAT'S THAT NUMBER?
MATHS FOCUS – NUMBER KIT 1

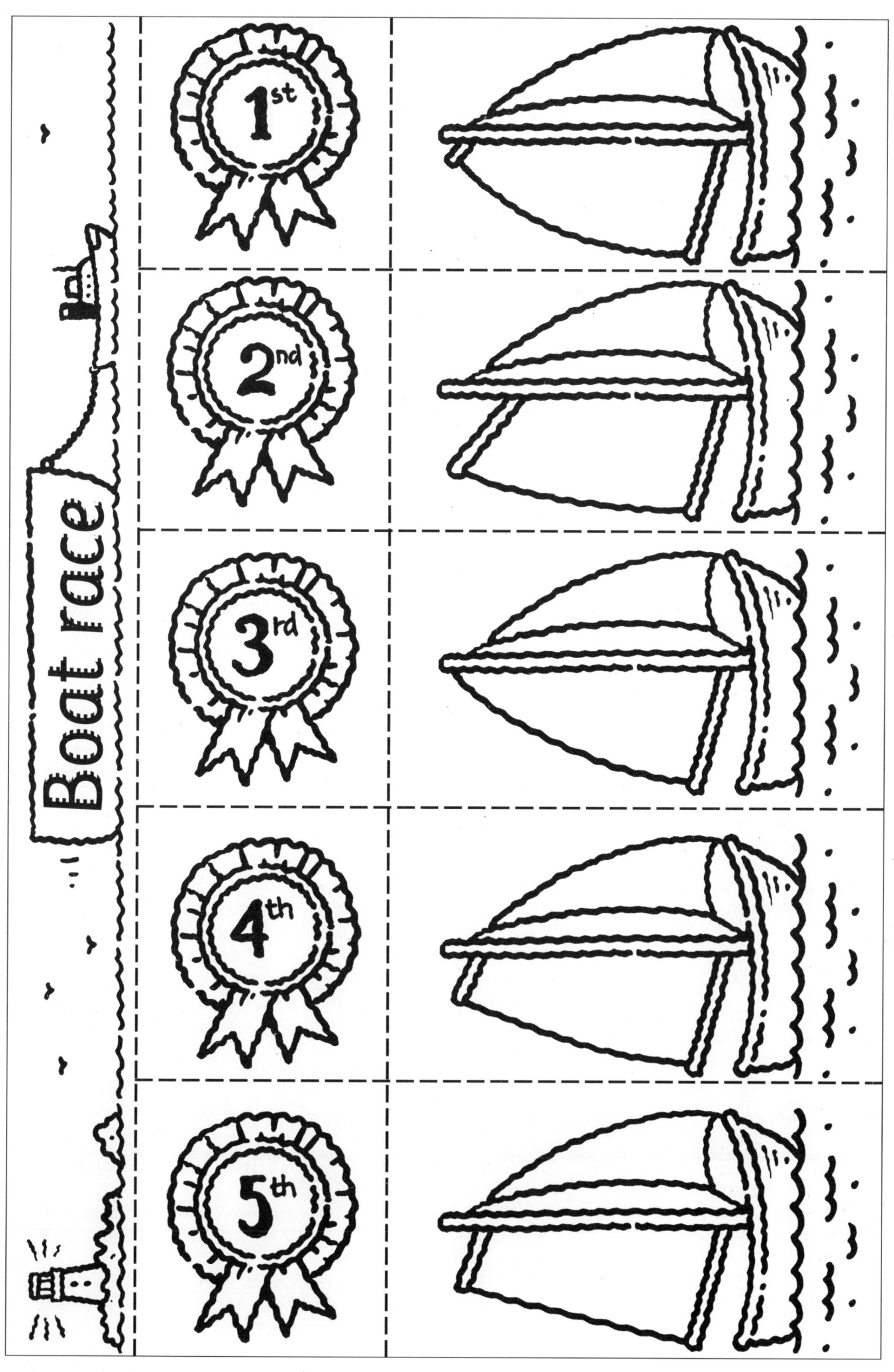

Boat race

1st
2nd
3rd
4th
5th

PHOTOCOPIABLE

WHAT'S THAT NUMBER?
MATHS FOCUS – NUMBER KIT 1

REINFORCEMENT ACTIVITY

Missing numbers

Key aim
◗ To develop the child's mental picture and knowledge of the order of numbers 1–10.

What you need
◗ 0–10 number cards (approximately A4 in size)
◗ 1 activity sheet per child
◗ 1 dice per child showing only one and two dots
◗ 1 small counter per child
◗ colouring pens and pencils

Introduction
◗ With the children in a line, fix one number card randomly to each child's clothing using masking tape. Tell the children that they are going to make a 0–10 'human' number line.
◗ Ask them to come up one by one, from the line, and try to 'get in order'. The child starting the number line may be wearing number 5. The next might be wearing number 7 and has to decide on which 'side' of number 5 to stand and so on.

The activity
◗ Give out the activity sheets and look at the first caterpillar. Let them fill in the missing numbers on their own. Check that they have all done this correctly before continuing.
◗ Now show them how to play the dice game.
◗ Tell them that they are to use the caterpillar on the bottom of their sheet. They start with their counter on the caterpillar's face, throw the 1–2 dice, move their counter on to the appropriate section of the caterpillar and write in the number. They continue until they reach the end of the caterpillar.
◗ They can use the first caterpillar to help them write in the correct number each time. Encourage them to count on from their previous number, for each go; for example, if they land on '2' initially then throw another '2' they count from 2 '3, 4'.
◗ Give them each a counter and dice and leave them to play.

Extension ideas
◗ Play the game again with a partner, taking it in turns to throw the dice and record the number.
◗ Play the game with more numbers, using the postermat.
◗ Draw the longest caterpillar they can with a number in each section, starting from 1.
◗ Make a class caterpillar for display on which the children can take turns to cover different sections for their friends to guess which number is underneath.

USING & APPLYING
PROBLEM SOLVING
◗ Use the first caterpillar to check answers.
◗ Work systematically.
COMMUNICATION
◗ Explain how to play the game to someone else.
◗ Talk about the position of the numbers.
LOGICAL REASONING
◗ Anticipate the next number.

TALK ABOUT
◗ 'What number should be in this space?'
◗ 'Which number comes after the one you've just landed on?'
◗ 'Which number comes before 6?'
◗ 'Which number comes in-between 7 and 9?'
◗ 'How many numbers are there between 5 and 8?'
◗ 'Which numbers haven't you landed on?'
◗ 'How did you use the first caterpillar to help you?'

HERE'S THE MATHS
◗ The children use their knowledge of the order of numbers to work out which number goes in each space on their caterpillar.

WHAT TO LOOK FOR
◗ Can the child not only see which numbers are missing but fill them in their correct space?

MORE HELP NEEDED
◗ Encourage the children to use the first caterpillar on their sheet to help them to check their answers.
◗ Children who have difficulty putting the missing numbers in sequence, need more activities on the order of numerals.

WHAT'S THAT NUMBER?
MATHS FOCUS – NUMBER KIT 1

Missing numbers

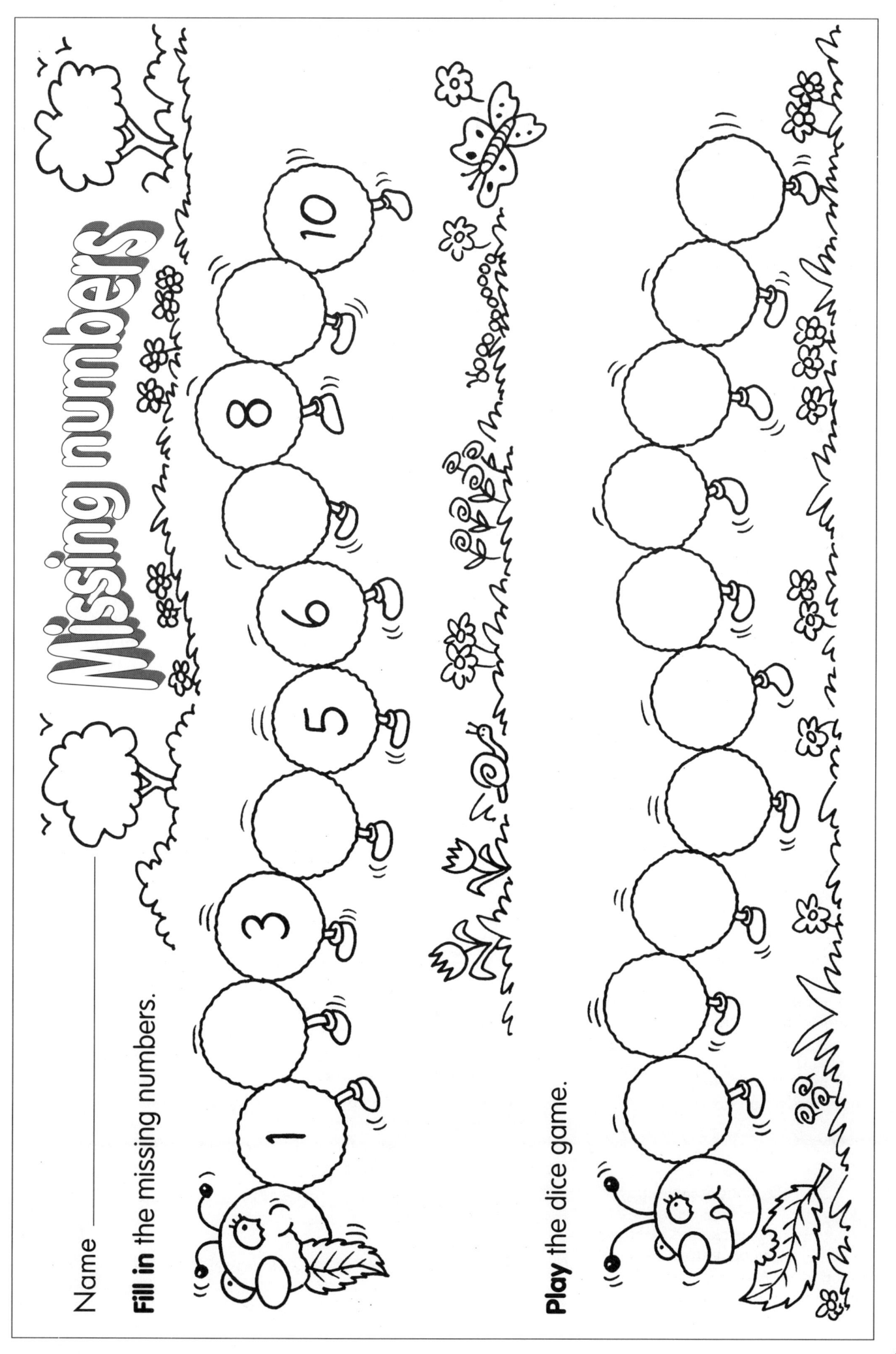

Name _____

Fill in the missing numbers.

1, __, 3, __, 5, 6, __, 8, __, 10

Play the dice game.

PHOTOCOPIABLE

WHAT'S THAT NUMBER?
MATHS FOCUS – NUMBER KIT 1

31

ENRICHMENT ACTIVITY

What a handful!

Key aims
▸ To develop a mental picture of a number of objects.
▸ To develop skills of estimation.
▸ **Also covered**: recording and writing numbers.

What you need
▸ variety of small objects for counting such as beans, beads, cubes, pasta
▸ 1 container for each type of object
▸ 1 activity sheet per child
▸ spare paper
▸ pens and colouring pencils

The activity
▸ Give out the activity sheets – and have one for yourself.
▸ Talk about the things in each of the containers. Pick a handful from one of the containers and ask the children to guess how many are in your hand – make sure they realise that you mean just to guess, and not to count the objects. Draw one of the objects on the first hand on your sheet.
▸ When they have all made a suggestion, say how many you think there are and write it in the 'guess' box on your sheet. Now count with the children how many there actually are and write the number in the 'count' box.
▸ Leave the children to complete the activity sheet on their own by picking a handful from one of the containers, guessing 'how many', recording their guess and then counting to check the actual number.

Extension ideas
▸ Working with a friend, let the children repeat the activity sheet both picking up the same 'things' each time. Compare guesses and results and think about why some answers may be different. You have a go picking up the same things, to make it even clearer that different-sized hands will be able to hold a different number of the object.
▸ Explore how different-sized containers will hold a different number of the same object.
▸ Collect the seeds from a sunflower or pumpkin to guess how many, then count.

USING & APPLYING
PROBLEM SOLVING
▸ Think about 'why' they are getting particular results.
COMMUNICATION
▸ Explain the difference between a guess and a count.
LOGICAL REASONING
▸ Make reasonable guesses.

TALK ABOUT
▸ 'Which guesses are close? How close?'
▸ 'Why have you picked up fewer pasta pieces than beads?'
▸ 'Why is your guess sometimes different from your count?'

HERE'S THE MATHS
▸ The children will be using their mental images of how small numbers are made up to make their estimates; for example, they may see a pattern of 3 and 4 in a group of seven objects.
▸ The 'Extension idea' activity counting sunflower seeds takes the children into bigger numbers, which they probably won't be able to count up to. However, it is good to stretch them and make them aware of the existence of bigger numbers. Let them group the seeds in 10s and then count the number of 10s there are.

WHAT TO LOOK FOR
▸ Can the child see patterns in small numbers?
▸ Can the child use her mental images of numbers to aid her counting?

MORE HELP NEEDED
▸ Children who have difficulty seeing patterns, and making sensible estimates, need more experience of number arrangements.

Name _____

What a handful!

A handful of: Guess   Count

ENRICHMENT ACTIVITY

Watch the numbers

Key aims
- To develop skills of observation and memory.
- To encourage the children to look closely at numerals.
- **Also covered**: encouraging an interest in what numbers look like.

What you need
- 1 activity sheet per child
- scissors
- envelopes

Organisation
- Provide an envelope in which each child can put his or her cards to take the game home to play.

The activity
- Give each child a copy of the activity sheet and ask them to cut up the number cards.
- Show them how to play the game:
• Place the number cards face down on the table and muddle them up. Player 1 picks up two cards.
• If the numbers match Player 1 keeps the pair and has another turn. If they do not match Player 1 puts the cards back in the same place face down on the table and the next player takes a turn.
• Continue taking turns until all of the cards have been picked up. The winner is the player with the most cards at the end of the game.

Extension ideas
- Tell one child to sort the numbers into different sets and ask their partner to guess the link.
- Make their own version of the game using a number line from which to select their numbers.

USING & APPLYING

PROBLEM SOLVING
- Understand the idea of the game in order to make a different version.

COMMUNICATION
- Talk about the numerals.

LOGICAL REASONING
- Identify and talk about which are the larger/smaller numbers.

TALK ABOUT
- 'Which numbers have a 3? Can you name them?'
- 'What is the same/different about some of the numbers?'

HERE'S THE MATHS
- The numbers in this activity are deliberately similar so that children have to identify significant features of the numbers to differentiate.
- When you ask the children what is the same/different about some of the numbers, they may notice that 12 and 21 both have a 1 and a 2 in them but in a different position. Although it is unlikely that they will know that one stands for the 10s the other for the units, it is important that they have such opportunities to extend their awareness of numbers.

WHAT TO LOOK FOR
- Can the child distinguish between all of the numbers in the way that they are written?

MORE HELP NEEDED
- Children who find difficulty distinguishing between, for example, 12 and 21, need more work looking closely at a number line and a number grid, and investigating the patterns and positions of the numbers.

Watch the numbers

12	12	3	10	10
21	21	3	20	20
9	9	13	15	15
19	19	13	25	25

✂ **Cut up** the number cards carefully.

USING & APPLYING

PROBLEM SOLVING
- Complete the task.
- Devise a different number line.

COMMUNICATION
- Discuss the numerals.

LOGICAL REASONING
- Discuss number patterns.

TALK ABOUT

- 'What number will be next?'
- 'What does 18 look like? Which way round does 5 go?'
- 'Can you count all the numbers you have made?'
- 'Do numbers stop at 30? If not how do they continue?'

HERE'S THE MATHS

- The children will be able to show the extent of their knowledge of the pattern and sequence of the order of numbers by creating number line tracks on the postermat which involve numbers as large as they know.

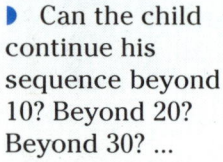

WHAT TO LOOK FOR

- Can the child continue his sequence beyond 10? Beyond 20? Beyond 30? ...
- Can the child see the pattern of each block of 10?

MORE HELP NEEDED

- Let those children having difficulty writing the numbers in order use the class number line to help them.
- Assess the extent of the child's ability to write numbers in order and provide the appropriate level of help, for example, reinforcing understanding of the teens numbers, helping them to see what becomes beyond 20.

ENRICHMENT ACTIVITY

Number lines

Key aims
- To work with larger numbers.
- To look at the repeating pattern in the order of numbers.

What you need
- number pieces (see 'Organisation')
- coloured arrows cut out from card
- Blu-Tack, masking tape or drawing pins
- colouring pens and crayons
- 1 activity sheet per child

Organisation
- Write out numbers up to 30 on a strip of card and cut these up into various arrangements of two or three numbers per piece. Let the children decorate each piece.

Introduction
- Give each pair one of the decorated number pieces. Decide on a starting point in the classroom and ask the pair with the first number piece to fix it at your agreed starting point.
- Ask them which number is needed next. Let the pair with this piece decide where in the classroom to fix it. Use the arrows to indicate from the first piece where this second piece can be found, for example, over a cupboard, around a corner.
- When it is complete count the numbers from start to finish.

The activity
- Tell the children that they are going to record the numbers from your class number line in the shape of a picture (with the numbers in sequence).
- Give them some examples, such as on a snake, a train with carriages, a caterpillar and so on.
- Leave them to create their picture number line on their activity sheet.

Extension ideas
- Continue their picture number line to 50 or 100.
- In pairs, use the postermat to make a number track, having different start numbers to go into larger numbers.

WHAT'S THAT NUMBER?
MATHS FOCUS – NUMBER KIT 1

Name _____

Number lines

How are you going to record your number line?

PHOTOCOPIABLE

USING & APPLYING

PROBLEM SOLVING
▶ Play the game correctly.
COMMUNICATION
▶ Talk about the numbers and direction of the move.
LOGICAL REASONING
▶ Be aware of the connection between moving forwards and '+' and moving backwards and '−'.

TALK ABOUT

▶ 'How many moves did it take to get to 20?'
▶ 'Jumping from 2 to 5 which numbers do you pass as you move?'
▶ 'Which button on the calculator moves you forwards?'
▶ 'Which button on the calculator moves you backwards?'

HERE'S THE MATHS

▶ The children are involved in linking addition and subtraction on the calculator to the moves they make. Some may be able to anticipate the calculator display by working it out in their heads first.
▶ This game provides a good introduction to subtraction being counting back, and doesn't have to involve children in understanding the concept of subtraction itself.

WHAT TO LOOK FOR

▶ Can the child count back from 20?
▶ Can the child use the calculator carefully, accurately and with understanding in relation to this activity?

MORE HELP NEEDED

▶ Children who have difficulty using the calculator need more experience of using it for free exploration, simple games and activities.

ENRICHMENT ACTIVITY

Rocket game

Key aims
▶ To give practice of going forwards and backwards along a number line.
▶ **Also covered**: using a calculator as part of the work.

What you need
▶ 1 activity sheet per pair
▶ 1 calculator per pair
▶ 1 counter per pair
▶ a set of number cards per pair (see page 46)
▶ pens/pencils

Organisation
▶ You may want to use a large display calculator when showing the children how to play the game.

The activity
▶ Give out the activity sheets. Talk about how countdowns are used when launching rockets. Together count from 0 to 20 and 20 to 0 following the numbers on the rocket.
▶ Show them the number cards (just the ones with '+' on) and tell them that the '+' sign means to move forwards.
▶ Explain how to play the game:
• Shuffle the number cards and put them face down in a pile.
• Set the calculator at zero and put your counter on zero.
• Player 1 turns over a number card and keys that operation and number into the calculator and moves the counter on to the appropriate section of the rocket.
• Player 2 does the same using the same calculator and moving the same counter.
• Play continues until you reach 20.
▶ Play the game again this time using subtraction cards to start at 20 and move back to 0. Explain that the '−' sign means to move back.

Extension ideas
▶ Think of a way to record their journey to 20 or 0.
▶ Start the game from 10 and use a mixture of addition and subtraction cards. One player aims to reach 20, the other to 0. On each turn decide whether to use or to pass the card.
▶ Write the numbers 0–30 on to the postermat (or a copy of page 48), and let the children use it with the cards to play a similar game, starting at the lighthouse.

WHAT'S THAT NUMBER?
MATHS FOCUS – NUMBER KIT 1

Name _____

Rocket game

| 20 |
| 19 |
| 18 |
| 17 |
| 16 |
| 15 |
| 14 |
| 13 |
| 12 |
| 11 |
| 10 |
| 9 |
| 8 |
| 7 |
| 6 |
| 5 |
| 4 |
| 3 |
| 2 |
| 1 |
| 0 |

PHOTOCOPIABLE

WHAT'S THAT NUMBER?
MATHS FOCUS – NUMBER KIT 1

39

ENRICHMENT ACTIVITY

Count forwards, count back

Key aims
- To explore order of numbers from various starting points.
- To help develop mental ordering of numbers.

What you need
- 1 activity sheet per child
- 1 postermat per pair
- dry-wipe markers and wiper

Organisation
- If you are using the photocopiable postermat (on page 48) you will need a number of copies for each pair.

Introduction
- Read the book *Ten, Nine, Eight* by Molly Bang (Red Fox). Collect and label each number of objects, put them in order and talk about what is happening to the numbers in the book.
- Count aloud from 10 back to 0 and from 0 forward to 10.
- Give the children a number and ask them to count forwards or back from that, for example: 'Start at 8... count back to 0'.

The activity
- Give each pair a copy of the postermat and show them how to write on and rub off.
- Ask them to choose any number and write it down on the lighthouse space and count forwards from that number, taking it in turns to write in the next number.
- They can then count backwards from the lighthouse to fill in the rest of the numbers in the chain. Wipe clean and repeat with a different number.
- When they have had time doing this give out the activity sheets. Tell them that the balls are part of a number chain. Leave them to work individually to fill in the missing numbers.

Extension ideas
- Start from any number on their postermat and complete the number chain going forwards and/or backwards. Rub out some numbers and swap with another pair and try to fill in each other's missing numbers.
- Devise their own game using the postermat. Decide on the rules and teach it to a friend.

USING & APPLYING
PROBLEMS SOLVING
- Apply own ideas to the task.
- Extend work.

COMMUNICATION
- Talk about the work and explain ideas clearly.

LOGICAL REASONING
- Choose equipment to make their own game and use it appropriately.

TALK ABOUT
- 'What number do you reach this time?'
- 'Why choose that number to start with?'
- 'When counting backwards do you always reach zero? If not, why not?'
- 'How would you fill in the numbers going forwards and backwards from that number?'
- 'What helps you find the missing numbers?'

HERE'S THE MATHS
- Children may understand the sequence of numbers to 10 but not realise there is a pattern that continues beyond that. Some have difficulty with the teens numbers, or haven't seen that there is a pattern in the repeated tens numbers. Help them to see these patterns.

WHAT TO LOOK FOR
- Can the child write the number after 5? 10? 19?
- Can the child write the number before 16? 21? 30?
- Can the child complete an incomplete number line to 20? 30? 100?

MORE HELP NEEDED
- Use this activity to assess which areas of number sequence a child has difficulty with so you can give specific help.

WHAT'S THAT NUMBER?
MATHS FOCUS – NUMBER KIT 1

Count forwards, count back

Fill in the missing numbers.

Name _____

PHOTOCOPIABLE

WHAT'S THAT NUMBER?
MATHS FOCUS – NUMBER KIT 1
41

ENRICHMENT ACTIVITY

Don't miss the train!

Key aim
◗ To build understanding and confidence in ordering numbers.

What you need
◗ a prepared class train (see page 47) and passengers
◗ 1 activity sheet per child
◗ plain paper, sticky tape, colouring pens and pencils

Organisation
◗ If you don't already have a class train, use the template on page 47 to make one from card, using multiple copies of the compartments. Each compartment should be a pocket in which each child can slot a picture of him/herself as they come into class each morning.

◗ Choose appropriate numbers for the number of passengers to fill in on each activity sheet according to each child's experience – they should at this stage be working with numbers 0–30 at least.

The activity
◗ Talk about the class train and explain that you want the children to draw their own trains for the number of passengers in the boxes on the activity sheet.
◗ When you are sure they understand what to do let them complete the activity sheet on their own.
◗ Let them use plain paper to continue their trains. Some children may want to join on other sheets of paper to extend their trains so they can fit all their carriages in one long line.

Extension ideas
◗ Give the children four different numbers representing the number of passengers for further trains which they can draw on the back of their sheet.
◗ Ask the child to draw passengers on each train, but to leave some compartments empty. Using a number line they can find out how many seats are filled and how many are empty.
◗ Challenge the children to draw the longest train they can and write on all the compartment numbers.

USING & APPLYING
PROBLEM SOLVING
◗ Draw the correct number of compartments.
◗ Record clearly and discuss recording used.
COMMUNICATION
◗ Discuss the work.

TALK ABOUT
◗ 'How many compartments do you need for this train?'
◗ 'How many passengers on this train?'
◗ 'Which is the longest train?'
◗ 'Which do you think will be the shortest train?'

HERE'S THE MATHS
◗ This activity relates the order of objects (first, second, third) with the sequence of numbers. Use the language of position with the children on as many occasions as possible.
◗ Use the train as a regular focus of class discussions. For example: ask the children how many people are on the train and how many compartments are empty on that particular day; ask them who is 1st... 3rd... 5th; challenge them to line up in order of the train to go to lunch.

WHAT TO LOOK FOR
◗ Can the child describe where in a sequence an object is, out of five objects? ten objects? ...

MORE HELP NEEDED
◗ Group and class discussions, with activities such as lining up in order, a sequence of actions in PE (this 1st, this 2nd ...) and so on, will help children who have difficulties with ordinal number.

WHAT'S THAT NUMBER?
MATHS FOCUS – NUMBER KIT 1

Don't miss the train!

Draw trains for this many passengers:

Name _____

Which is the longest train? _____

Which is the shortest train? _____

PHOTOCOPIABLE

WHAT'S THAT NUMBER?
MATHS FOCUS – NUMBER KIT 1

43

Name _____

Fish around a number

44 WHAT'S THAT NUMBER?
MATHS FOCUS – NUMBER KIT 1

PHOTOCOPIABLE

Dotty numbers cards

To cut out and play with.

Name _____

Instructions: Shuffle the cards and place them face down on a table. Players take turns to pick up two cards. Keep the cards if the number and dots match, if not turn them back over and it is the next player's turn. The player with the most cards at the end wins.

1	•	6	•• •• ••
2	••	7	••• •• ••
3	•••	8	•• •• •• ••
4	•• ••	9	••• ••• •••
5	•• • ••	10	••• ••• •• ••

PHOTOCOPIABLE

WHAT'S THAT NUMBER?
MATHS FOCUS – NUMBER KIT 1
45

Rocket game

+4	+4	+4	+4
+3	+3	−3	−3
+2	+2	−2	−2
+1	+1	−1	−1

Don't miss the train!

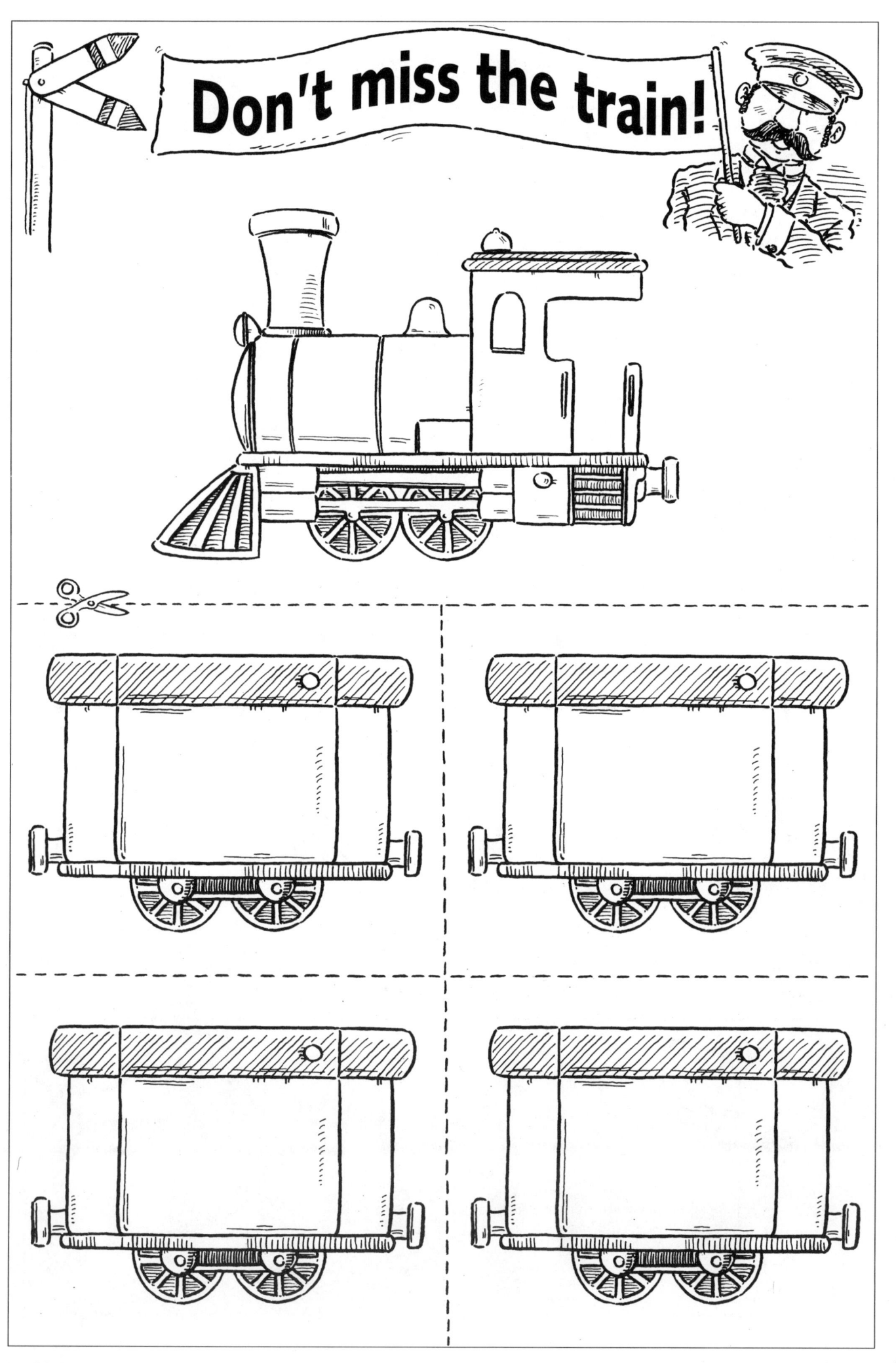

PHOTOCOPIABLE

WHAT'S THAT NUMBER?
MATHS FOCUS – NUMBER KIT 1

48 WHAT'S THAT NUMBER?
MATHS FOCUS – NUMBER KIT 1

PHOTOCOPIABLE